The Gathering:
Stones for the Medicine Wheel

For Jeff, who wasn't afraid to challenge me.
Sandy, who gave me the courage.
And for D.A., who, like the Medicine Wheel,
left behind a mystery.

The Gathering:
Stones for the Medicine Wheel

Gregory A. Scofield

POLESTAR
BOOK PUBLISHERS
VANCOUVER / WINLAW

The Gathering : Stones for the Medicine Wheel

Second Printing, 1996

Polestar Book Publishers
Second Floor, 1011 Commercial Drive
Vancouver, British Columbia, V5L 3X1
(604) 251-9718

Canadian Cataloguing in Publication Data
Scofield, Gregory, 1966–
The gathering:

Poems.
ISBN 0-919591-74-4

1. Title.
PS8587.C63G3 1993   C811'.54   C93-091001-X
PR9199.3.S36G3   1993

Acknowledgements
Published with the assistance of the Canada Council and the
British Columbia Cultural Services Branch

Cover design and illustration by Jim Brennan
Author photograph by Mark Richfield
Cree translation of *Black Bear's Grandson* by Freda Ahenakew
Interior illustrations by Jim Brennan
Interior production by Julian Ross & GoldRush Type & Graphics
Printed and bound in Canada

Contents

West / Arrival

North / Searching

East / Dreams

South / Healing

kaskitêw-maskwa osisima

aya kayâs, ê-mêkwâ-pipohk, kaskitêw-maskwa kîkway ê-kî-mây-âpahtahk. nîso ê-wâpamât ocawâsimisa acahkw-askîhk ê-wî-isi-sipwêhtahimiht, êkwa ê-kakîsimostawât kisê-manitowa kiyâm êkâ nânitaw ka-ispayiyit okosisa.

êkosi kisê-manitow kinwês ma-mâmitonêyihtam, ê-ati-sîkwâk êkwa wîhtamawêw kaskitêw-maskwa, «nikosis,» itêw, «mistahi mihcêt kîkway kipê-miyitin, êwako pêyak ôma, ka-isi-nanâtawhihat otahkosiw. piko ka-miyiyan kikosisak êkosi onîsokâtêw-iyiniw tâkîsâkaskinahtâw watay. êkâ kisiwâsi, kî-pê-âyimanipipon êkwa kî-pê-kino-pipon.»

êkosi ispayin kisê-manitow kâ-kî-tasiwêt, kaskitêw-maskwa koskonêw okosisa êkwa itohathêw okosisa ka-nitaw-minihkwêyit, ka-mîcisoyit êkwa ka-kisîpêkinastêyit. ê-pôn-âpihtâ-kîsikâyik êkwa têpwâtêw okosisa ê-wîhtamawât tânisi ê-wî-itahkamikisit.

«nikosisak,» itêw, «piko kwêyask ka-nitohtamêk. êkâya pimitisahok ôma kâ-wî-mâcîyân. wêtinahk ma-mêtawêk, êkwa takohtêyâni ka-miyawâtênânaw ê-sîkwâk.»

êkosi ohtâwîwâwa ê-kî-itikocik ôki nîso oskinîkiwak ma-mêtawêwak iskohk ê-ati-tipiskâyik. nanatatohk kîkway pêhtâkwan iyiw êkwa tipiskâw-pîsimwa ê-sâkêwêyit êkwa kahkiyaw kîkway cakastêhtin iyiw, êkosi kwayask ati-sêkisiwak oskinîkiwak êkosi ati-sipwêhtêwak ê-nitaw-nitonawâcik ôhtâwîwâwa.

namoya kinwêsk âsay nohtêhkatêwak êkwa nêstosiwak. êkosi ostêsimâw ê-moyêyihtahk osîmisa ê-nêstosiyit, kîsêyihtam ka-nakîcik. cîki êkota sakâsiniyiw, êkota nahisinwak ê-wî-nipâcik.

iyikohk ê-nêstosicik namoy ahpo pêhtawêwak

omâcîwa ê-pêtwêwênamiyit. kâ-pêkopayicik êkwa
awêsôma kî-ayâwak acâhkwaskîhk. kihtwâm ê-
otâkosik, mitoni miyawatamwak nîsokâtakêw-iyini-
wak.

mihcêt askiy êkwa, kaskitêw-maskwa ê-ati-kêhtê-
ayiwit êkwa ê-ati-nêsowisit, kêyâpic nanâtawihêw
otahkosiwa. mihcêtwâw mâna kiskisiw okosisa êkwa
ayiwâk ati-kaskêyimêw okosisa tahtw-âskiy.

âsay mîna kihtwâm ê-ispayik wawêyistam ka-
nitaw-ayiwêpit êkosi. kaskitêw-maskwa wîpac kî-kway-
asitêw owâtihk ê-wî-kakwê-nitaw-nipât.

kî-pîhtwâtâwêw otôspwâkana, ê-kâkîsimotawawât
kisê-manitowa êkâ êwakoyikohk ka-nipahêyihtahk.

ê-ati-nîpiniyik âsay mîna kisê-manitowa kâ-
pawâtât, «nikosis,» itik, «kâkikê ki-pê-kistêyimin, kiya
mâwaci ê-pê-kihcêyimiyan, êkosi ka-miyitin kîkway:
pâh-pêyak kikosisak ohci. nistam ôma, têpakohp ôki
kihcihtawâw-asiniyak the Great Medicine Wheel
kîsikohk.»

«êkwa ôma kotak kâ-wî-miyitân,» itik. «êwako
osisimâw. namoy ôma tâpiskoc ôki kikosisak, mâka
onîsokâtêw-iyiniw. ka-kiskinahamawâw kimaskaw-
isîwin êkwa mîna asinîyak ôki osohkâtisiwiniwâw.»

êkosi kâkî-isi-asotamâkot kaskitêw-maskwa kisê-
manitowa, ê-pêkopayit êkota têpakohp kihcîhtwâw-
asiniya kî-apiyiwa. mihcêtwâskiy ê-kî-kakwê nisito-
htawât, ka-kiskinahamâkot ôhi asiniya okiskina-
hamâkêwiniyiwa. êkosi tahk-âyiwâk ati-sohkisiw awa
otînihkahiwêw, tahk-âyiwâk mistahi ê-ati-itêyimikot
pisiskiwa êkwa mîna nîsokâtêw-iyiniwa.

pêyakwâw ê-otakosik kaskitêw-maskwa ê-mêkwa-
ayiwêpit, pêyak oskinîkiw kâ-pê-pihtokwêt, pôt ôma

nîsokâtêw-iyiniwa wêscakâsiyiwa ê-osâwâyiki tâpiskôc
nîpiya kâ-takwâkik êkwa oskîsikwa tâpiskôc. waskway
kâ-nîpîhk.

«nôsisim,» itêw kaskitew-maskwa, «âstam ôta pê-
wa-wîtapimin cîki kotawânihk ka-wâpahtihitin ôki
kihcihtwâw-asiniyak.» kaskitêw-maskwa ê-môsahkinât
ê-kâh-kitâpamât wêtinahk; «awa akiniy,» itêw, «awa
asiniy êwakw âwa kiya mêmohc, êkwa awa asiniy, niya,
êkwa awa nisto asiniy kikâwînak, êkwa nêwo kôhtâwî-
nawak, êkwa awa niyânan asiniyw,» itwêw. «kimisi-
nawak, êkwa awa nikotwâsik asiniy, kistêsinawak, êkwa
awa têpakohp asiniy, kahkiyaw pisiskowak.»

«ôki asiniyak,» itwêw kaskitêw-maskwa,
«êwakonik ôki mîna asiniyak ê-apîstahkik ayamihâwin,
kahkiyaw okimâwiwin, nihtâwêyihtamowin, êkwa
kahkiyaw misiwêskamik The Great Medicine Wheel
ôki ê-ohcipayicik ôki asiniyak, êkwa kahkiyaw kîkway
pâh-pahkân pêyakwan ê-itakihtêk êkota pihcâyihk
kihci-wawiyêyâw. kahkiyaw kîkway miyo-wîcêhtô-
makan êkwa mîna nîsokatêw-iyiniw.»

kaskitêw-maskwa mihcêtwâskiy kî-kiskina-
hamawêw ôsisima ôhi ohci asiyiniya.

ispi êkwa ê-nakataskêt kaskitêw-maskwa âsay êkwa
osisima mistahi kiskêyihtamawin ayâyiwa, mâka
kêyâpic namoya mitoni kîsi-nisitohtawêyiwa ôhi
asiniya. âsay êkwa ê-kî-pôni-pimâtisit kaskitêw-
maskwa kî-pawâtik ôsisima, «nôsisim, kikî-miyitin
nimaskawisîwin êkwa nikiskêyitamowin mâka kêyâpic
kit-ôsk-ayiwin êkwa kêyâpic mistahi ka-nitaw-kiskêyi-
htaman. êkwa kipimâtisiwinihk nîyâk kika-wâpahtên
ê-âyimahk, mâka mîna mistahi ka-wâpahtên mîywêyi-
htamowin. piko ka-nitohtawat kitêh, cikêma êkota

kika-miskên tâpwêwin. misiwêskamik ka-pa-pâmâci-
hon êkwa âskaw ka-wanikiskisitotawin êkwa ka-
wanikiskisin mîna nikiskinahamâkêwina. mâka
nôsisim, piko ka-nitaw-môsahkinacik asinîyak, êkwa
nôsisim, ôki piko asiniyak kâkikê kâ-pimâtisicik.»

—Cree translation by Freda Ahenakew

Black Bear's Grandson

Long ago, in the season when all is sleeping, Black Bear received a disturbing vision. In this vision, he saw that his two young sons would be taken to the spirit world. Distraught, he prayed to the Great Spirit, pleading for them to be spared.

The Great Spirit thought for a long while, and in the spring gave Black Bear his decision. "My son," he replied, "I have given you many great things; among them, the power to cure sickness. You must let me take your sons so that the Two-Leggeds can fill their empty stomachs. Do not be angry, for it has been a long and difficult winter."

So as the Great Spirit had instructed, Black Bear woke his sons and took them to the river to drink, eat and bathe. At mid-afternoon, he called them together and told them of his plans.

"Little ones," he began, "you must listen closely. Do not follow me while I am hunting. Play quietly among yourselves, for when I return we shall celebrate the waking of spring."

So as their father had requested, the brothers played until evening fell. Strange sounds filled the night and they became afraid. The moon had risen, casting eerie shadows along the shoreline, thus the brothers ventured off into the darkened forest in search of their father.

Before long, the brothers grew hungry and tired. The eldest, sensing his brother's weariness, decided to stop. A few feet away lay a sparsely-wooded grove in which the pair curled up to sleep. They were so tired, they did not hear the hunter's approaching footsteps. When they awoke, they were in the land of the spirits. The following evening, there was much rejoicing in the village of the Two-Leggeds.

Many years passed and Black Bear, now old and weary, contined to heal the sick. He often thought of his lost sons and his heart grew lonelier with each passing season.

Again came another sleeping season and Black Bear retired to his den early, preparing himself for his long rest. He smoked the sacred pipe, praying that the Great Spirit take away his loneliness.

Late in the season, the Great Spirit came to him in another vision. "My son," he said, "over the years you have honoured me greatly. You are the most loyal of all my children and, for this, I will give you two gifts: one for each of your sons. My first gift is seven sacred stones from the Great Medicine Wheel in the sky. Listen to them closely, for they will teach you many powerful things."

"My second gift," he continued, "will be a grandson. He will not be in the form of your sons, but a young Two-Legged. Teach him your strength and the power of the stones."

And so as the Great Spirit had promised, Black Bear woke to find the seven sacred stones. He spent many years studying them, listening reverently to their teachings. He grew to be even more of a powerful healer, gaining respect from the other animals as well as the Two-Leggeds.

One evening, while Black Bear was resting, a young man appeared in his den. He was unlike any other Two-Legged Black Bear had seen. His hair was the colour of autumn leaves, and his eyes, blue like the summer sky.

"Grandson," Black Bear called, "come sit with me

by the fire and I will show you these sacred stones."
Black Bear gathered them up, examining them
thoughtfully. "This stone," he began, "represents you.
And this one, me. The third stone represents our
mothers. The fourth, our fathers. The fifth stone," he
continued, "our sisters. The sixth, our brothers. And
lastly, the seventh stone, the animal kingdom."

"These stones," he continued, "also represent reli-
gions, governments, philosophies, and entire nations.
They come from the Great Medicine Wheel in the sky,
and all things are equal within its sacred circle. The
circle is our total universe. Everything except the Two-
Leggeds are harmonious within it."

Black Bear spent many years teaching his grandson
about the stones. By the time of his passing, the young
man had learned many things. But still, he did not
fully understand the stones.

On the eve of Black Bear's death, he came to his
grandson in a dream and told him, "Grandson, I have
given you my strength and knowledge. Because you are
still young, there is much to learn. In your lifetime, you
will experience many hardships. But also, there will be
much happiness. You must always listen to your heart,
for it is there you will find truth and meaning. You will
journey many places, often forgetting me and my
teachings. But now, grandson, you must go and gather
your stones. For only the stones live forever."

West / Arrival

Dreams in Neon

Coyote Tricks

Coyote's up to tricks again
Works his keemootch ways
In dreams
Chase me backwards laughing.
Kiyas
I left this place
Cold and barren
Houses occupied by ghosts
Restless, chained to memories of grandfather's drum
How it beat against my plans

Echo the empty streets
And coyote's howling down
A neon sky
Transforms to a wino gone snaky
Would have sold his spirit for the real stuff;
The stuff that makes you forget
How the wind whispered.
Kiyas
I left that day
Suitcase in hand.

Whisky Burns

whisky burns goin' down
gets easier after the first swallow
rumblin' my frozen guts   warm up those trappin'
stories   how I slaved the whole winter to pay my Bay
bill—sidetracked that bartender talkin' tradin' lingo
caught his greedy eyes smoothin' over beaver pelts
nicely tanned; my woman's
fingers molded to the shape of her fleshin' tool
said I'd get some decent boots next winter
second swallow   real hot inside
third   loose my moshom's pocket watch
fourth   just gets easier goin' down

Barter Tongue

Not so easy doin' a kohkum's job: up all night
Pushin' a needle.
Takes patience to steady fingers, manoeuvre
Beads into place. Impress myself. These baby
Moccasins look like her work.

Throw in braid ties and keychains for fifty.
Get thirty if I'm lucky.
Smoothing my barter tongue is an entirely
different craft.
Only natural to put on my bush accent.
That dealer likes to think
He's supporting a dying art   not to mention
A dying race.
Hey, that's fine by me. I work damn hard for my
drinkin' money.
Would give her a good chuckle
If I took up bingo.

Last Night's Rebellion

Up too early
Breakfast of coffee and cigarettes
Somewhere drifting
The whine of a steel guitar
Or is it a fiddle?

Fresh snowfall
Erases last night's goings-on
At the Avenue Hotel
Jigging til my moccasins blew a hole—Okay,
I got another pair.

Up too early
Fist connecting to cheekbone
Still hurts
Could have been worse
At least I said my piece: To hell with you!
We never lost Batoche or Seven Oaks.

Welfare Lady

Elevated so high
A five-figured queen
Safe
Ruling her concrete queendom
Looking down on me
Would be easier just to die
Crawl inside
Forget

Just imagine her royal throne
Under the Georgia Viaduct
Scrounging her lunch from a dumpster
Behind the hotel
Drunk on her own power
The power of being a damn good scavenger

Cashing in those beer bottles
Bring just enough to howl tonight
Closing time—loving time
Cosy up to her old king
Making her forget tomorrow
And that appointment at ten

Different Loads

Here on the West Coast we got our own place.
Claiming a park downtown is simple—pass out on a
Bench. No hang-ups when it comes to stringing our
Rags in public. Hang-out darks with whites. You either
Come from the same hamper or you don't.

Uptown whites are an entirely different load. They
Get stained behind closed doors, at cocktail parties
Or business luncheons. Moving along their corporate
Clothesline you got to have a certain satin appeal—
Burlap wear. One day you get the permanent press
Treatment—the next you're bounced.

Indians got the right idea. An old wringer washer does
One hell of a good job. Who needs a dry cleaner to
Keep secrets? We share ours come washing day.

Big-Time Poaching

Big-time poaching
In a downtown beer joint
Mooching this white guy
So impressed
I'm a bonafide road-kill scavenger
Triggers his latest hunting adventure
Up north
Turned out a wasted trip; those moose
Are gettin' a whole lot smarter.

Ah, Indian knowledge
Start my mind thinkin' like an ancient
Hunter
Squinted eyes so deep in thought   Give
Just enough time to order up another
Pitcher

Careful now not to blow my cover
Sippin' slow   Work him into the clearing
Load-up   Take aim
Shoot: must be Indians tippin' them off.

Urban Dwelling

From My E. 6th Balcony

A heavy sky wraps around me
suffocating sunlight disappears too early
It's the factory billowing day & night
making black spots on our lungs
These rush-hour ants are oblivious
racing mechanically over the bridge
they don't know shortcuts take longer getting home
I can't think with all these horns blaring
only the usual city hum can I tune out after dark
Dangerous predators own the streets
hungry to taste some action
what feast they missed out on since last night
I dreamt of an ancient Hopi adobe, meditating
on rooftop, I watched the Kachina dancers circling
beneath a vibrant, cleansing sky.

What a Way to Go

Middle of the month
  We're so hard pressed
    Hunting through every pocket

Hoping I stashed
  A little something away
    Teasing gum wrappers show up

My lucky prize jingling
  Deep down between the lining
    Escaped coins just frustrate

What is her majesty
  Doing for supper tonight?
    Fry bread sounds good

We might have moose
  If we were bush Indians
    But our appetite is city cuisine

Back home our elders
  Have ancient taste buds
    Wintertime they stock up

Long distance hunting stories
  Confirm who is a good grandson
    Staying put keeping freezers filled

Coming together to feast
  It all seems so simple
    Taking from the land, being thankful

In the city we hunt each other
  Looking to borrow some flour, sugar, tea
    Just enough to get by til the end of the month

One Tough Skin Sister

Her face looks like it's been through a meat grinder.
Coming off a wine drunk, it looks even worse. She
should be six feet under, at least one foot buried

but some unseen power gave her nine lives. Probably
a goddamned man too, she adds. I don't blame her.
Her mouth is still pretty swollen: purple-red lips
without expression

tho when going on about finally getting electricity
up north, she squeezes out a joke—how pissing in
the dark you needed a seeing-eye dog.

Getting a one-way to the coast was a smart move. The
only drawback, her grand-kids. Hard to imagine her
being a granny, howling her warsong through chipped
teeth, telling how all those smart-assed brothers
wore out their sorry welcome.

When It Come to Your Turn

Your stink mouth shows
I'm the history lesson
You flunked in school
Too stoned to comprehend
You got your street degree
Bashing in some squaw's face
Made you a hero in this town
Would be pointless for me to move
Even to Utopia
My job would be the same
I'd hang around the liquor store, say,
Buddy, you got sum change?
So when it comes to your turn
Come to Indian country
Pull up a beer—start that
White mouth running
Guaranteed
You'll leave speechless

Nothing Sacred

Excavate: uproot a granny
                     gets a new resting place   pay
                     five bucks to view her in a
                     plexiglass tomb

New Age Movement: b & e our healing lodge
                     making off with our medicine
                     bird   so much for your
                     exhausted Buddha on the altar

Fashion: Pocahontas makes Vogue in
                     that two-piece buckskin
                     trim your fantasy with fringe
                     and beads   feathers tacky

Tourist Traps: only place to get a genuine
                     Wong & Sons totem pole
                     deciphering clan designs
                     extra

Read All About It: Pigeon Park Indians make
                     Premier an honorary drinking
                     chum   big powwow
                     scheduled after party

For Now: steal our spotlight   his high
                     profile   mixing promises
                     and Lysol

Jungle Cure

After dark those jaguar eyes hunger for more
Stalking street jungle   Up   Down
Backwards   Honing in
Spot their prey
Extending razor claws

Get a good grip tonight
In a room, a backseat   Scrunched for space
Stretch over this way, gazelle
Want to admire that exotic area
Between nipples

Something's up when they do that
Each mouthful inches closer to the jugular
Best to meditate yourself to another scene:
Up north is always soothing, just concentrate
On waves crashing

Once the bleeding stops, you're okay—those
Raw patches will heal before next week
They'll get safari fever, need a jungle cure

Survival Poetry

Down here there is a different kind of poetry
Not classical poetry
With smooth & eloquent verse
Not even love poetry
Taking you to some far-off gazebo by crashing waves
But survival poetry
Raw, unflinching
Watching your back in some skid row bar
Down here
Each line will give you a day—or make it your last

North / Searching

A Place to Start

Seemed to be the best place to start
Spending the day in Little Italy
Looking over a sea of faces
Hoping to spot him in a cappuccino bar
Or deli
No luck   I didn't have that swarthy look

Going to the skids
Felt more natural—like coming home
Could see him working deals   Drinking
With Skin brothers
Tho he could have easily passed for white

In his three-piece suit   Uptown
Playing another role: the businessman roll
Got him two years   More like
An entire lifetime
Sorting my grandmother's recollections
How he called us kids Bambino
A good cover   Being he probably joined the
Native Brotherhood inside

Just Medicine

Someone got even on that old bugger
held up on crutches
making his way into town
dragging his bum leg behind
those support boots look so heavy
swollen-up feet cursing inside
not the same gutter language
I remember going over my head
but I knew F meant something nasty
he got his sleazy thrills
liking the feel of each dirty word
my mom did her shopping quickly

Paying half down on a bottle
she was good for it so no problem
except the usual free sample
only one because I tagged along
making sure she came home
I was her little watchdog
ready to attack if he got too cheeky
he just sat there minding his p's & q's
tho in his later years
he must have gotten greedy for a touch
running up against some powerful shawoman
into bad medicine

Saint Mother

for Bernard Kabatow

She made an occupation out of keeping other
Women's children   flawless   Even bone china
Looked cheap up against that keemootch smile

Those social workers had some nerve making
Her a saint   Mother Teresa would have spit
If she knew about that cashy advance   Taking

Me in   What did I know about Christian duty
I was a wild Indian fresh from the slums
Defacing her neighbourhood   making a tipi

Out back   I had this thing for authenticity
Westerns were my favorite   I wanted a mini
Village   to be the chief   not her idea of

Civilization   tho a haircut made me look
Tame
She couldn't break me like her other kids

Taste of Hatred

I was too young
hearing that word Aryan
my first taste of hatred
I groaned my way through
Alex Haley's
ROOTS

cross burnings & Amazing Grace
left me cringing
I had to ask my mom
what is a nigger?
White people's fear, she said
we all bleed red blood

but who could believe that after
reading about the Holocaust
even those ghastly pictures
were no guarantee
that fascist purity wouldn't
soil every generation

back then, how easy for me
hating every pale face
I was all Indian
listening to Buffy St. Marie
chanting my history
downtown

the worst I saw
in Vancouver up close
one of my own
slugging his wife for booze money
her broken look
filled my mouth with bile

The Last Time I Saw Nimis

for Irene Awasis

The days, the hours change far too quickly.
Just yesterday, she was up wanting a smoke,
better food. Rushing home, I was back by
dinnertime with hard-boiled eggs, bannock
with jam. For a moment, nothing had changed.
She teased me by saying I'd make someone a
good wife.

The April sunshine doesn't belong here, or
maybe it's the other way around? She needs
to be outside, away from this room. If I
had my way, we'd be sitting in the hills,
laughing about the time Dale made me recite
my first full sentence in Cree. You would
say, "Poor white thing." But this time, I
wouldn't act so hurt.

The antiseptic smell, the disinfectants seep
into my mind, lodging a new memory in heart.
Each visit—every word straining takes more
than I have. Occasionally, she joins us in
the living, thoughts all jumbled. But death
closes in; invades her body, leaving behind
a shell from a prehistoric past. I knew
I couldn't be there for her last breath.
She'll be waiting to razz me about it.

Talking Because I Have To

When first I saw rye whisky
get the worst of him
he was smashing everyone in sight.
Hearing my mother scream, I ran downstairs.
My kiddy voice was no match.
She just lay there, convulsing under his
boots.

My mouth still knows what happened:
puffed-up lips I remember.
The rest is hazy, a long-ago movie. Someone
yells, "Go to the neighbours, call the cops."
And it ends there

Leaving a disturbed feeling over the years.
Even now, they say, "Greg, forget it."
Going on is made easier because they won't
talk. I talk because I have to.

Thinking of Father on this Day

Everyone is sitting down for dinner; presents given.
A clown's tie comes to mind, maybe some tools for
The garage? A wrench seems so hard, unfeeling.

The mountains divide us neatly,
as good an excuse as any.
Having been to Winnipeg once, I thought about
The lost years. There are lots of Cree & Saulteaux
Filling-up the city—mostly
Vacant-eyed kids.

Counting the scarring years, the jagged father-figures:
I could have easily become an island, stayed hidden.
Saying I should forget every fist, each hateful
Mouthful is to say I deserved it all. Even now, this
Day takes work: catch myself wondering how it might
Have been different if he'd stuck around.

Deceiving Honour

What do I owe her honour, a life
story that kept her mouth busy?
How easy to impress me, making
relations in a peyote ceremony.
K Mart clothes sealed new blood
ties; ever a sneaky way how she
worked.

Her rush training me to act the
proper son left me thinking we
should be married. She didn't
want to hear my troubles, just my
sex life. I needed to
expose old lovers, put down the
bottle, attend more ceremonies.

She would have done well running
a residential school. The whole
family confessed on themselves.
They sat around gloomy, awaiting
her priestly wisdom. I was too
stubborn. Her ulcer was a good
excuse, blaming me for being too
private.

She wanted to put up an undoing
ceremony. Damn smart move, that
got me talking. Everywhere she
went she spread my dirt. Years
later, seeing her at a powwow,
I pitied her.

Divided

My beigey-pink shade
Unlike you with bronze skin
I'm a Skin without colour; I get the brushoff
Ego-tripping on me again
Deciding if I am pure enough   Red enough
To be whole but the whole of me says
Enough of this colour crap
I am not your white whipping-boy

Growing up in an all-white town
I never forgot my red half   It counted big
Especially if you looked not right white
But wrong white   To white people that's off-white
Dirty white in Sally Ann clothes
You got followed in stores
They just asked a lot if you needed help   Not help
To find the right size but to the door   To the cop shop
If you got caught stealing
That was it   no second chance
They just nailed your raggedy ass to the wall
Never mind in school
You kept your head down   Ducked the put-downs
Shoved it all down

Between Me 'n' Hank

Something to be proud of   a hand-to-mouth existence
Growing up moaning along with Hank Williams
I learned the blues first-hand
Even tho it was from another era
Poverty looks the same in every generation
Only I didn't know the half of it
Like my mom, my aunt
They were the real unsung heroes
Making something out of nothing
I always got my fair share   even more
When I think about it
He must have had a strong halfbreed mother

History

I can say what I am, a little too cheeky
And keep my grudge nose in place.

It's history. At the Hudson's Bay taking
Inventory; these blankets weren't worth
Chasing beavers.

They itch like hell, remind me I'm still
Too sensitive. Still, I want a red one with
Black stripes,

Four points equal 2 beaver, 1 fox, 3 mink.
How handy it must be bartering with plastic,
Just say, "Charge it."

But I can't even afford the escalator ride.
These white people smell so rich. I need a
New look to go with my free sample.

Keeping it simple, cheap—
Browsing the Sally Ann you find all kinds of
Treasures.

My place looks like a trading post
For half the price; I'm giving old Rupert a
Run for his money.

God of the Fiddle Players

The wilting sun catches them centre stage, taking a
Well-deserved breather. Safely shielded by the big top,
Easy for me to applaud for more. An old-timer's
Favorite, my mom would say.

Surveying the dance floor, my generation is damn-near
Lost. Even me, I don't know how to promenade
Properly, let alone that quick heel-toe-on-the-spot
Step. Gyrating to a techno-beat is more my history.
Then again, who can dig roots in the city?

I have to ask a friend about being Métis, what there is
To be proud of. Because she's an elder, she says just
Watch, listen. Later, we join the pilgrimage to the
Graveyard, go to the museum.

They have a special show using mannequins to
Re-enact the Northwest Resistance. Weeping openly, I
Got to meet the heroes I was ashamed of in school.

That summer, the God of the Fiddle Players visited
Batoche. I bought my first sash; wearing it proudly
Around the house, practicing the ins & outs of jigging.

Eli

His voice a harp to soothe my childhood fears
  so long ago
this memory of you & me hidden out back
  peering down from the safety of our maple tree
waiting out the drunken rages—pretending we didn't
hear the ashtrays crashing—singing to silence
  the screams
of glass cutting a mother's
delicate flesh.

Eli, where did you vanish to when I was fifteen?
  Only an image remained:
coal-black hair, deep wells of brown where I drew my
strength, love. But these too became another memory;
  fleeting with the years like the wings of a bird
  ascending higher, higher until gone.

Who will know these ancient scars, except you & me?
Even the streets, the human replacements
could not silence your playing, how you once lulled me
to sleep.

Call Me Brother

"You never know when you're talking to an Indian," he
says wisely because I am only half which we both know
is not the real issue but the way I look which makes it
next to impossible not to spot me sticking out at a
powwow because I have the tourist look that offends
my darker relations who don't see me as related but a
wannabe muzzling up around the drum to sing 49ers
except I feel the beat like my own heart racing when
curious eyes study if I am just mouthing the words or
actually belting them out because I am a true die-hard
Skin with blue eyes that really screws up the whole
history book image except my roots can't be traced to
the Bering Straight but nine months after European
contact which to this day hasn't been forgiven even
tho we all have some distant grandpa who at one time
or another took an Indian wife which we tend to forget
because anything but pure is less than perfect and we
all secretly need someone to be better than so the
next time you see me up dancing call me brother

East / Dreams

Kohkum's Lullaby

Kiya mato noosisim
Kiya mato
Kiya mato

Kosim'mow nichimoose
Kosim'mow
Kosim'mow

Tome'pah noosisim
Tome'pah
Tome'pah

Sakehi'tin nichimoose
Sakehi'tin
Sakehi'tin

Don't cry grandchild
Don't cry
Don't cry

Lay down sweetheart
Lay down
Lay down

Go to sleep grandchild
Go to sleep
Go to sleep

I love you sweetheart
I love you
I love you

Shadow Dreaming

What does this dream mean, a warning?
Something inside me has changed.
I'm moving far too cautiously, seeing
More than I want to.
Searching for a shadow in daylight
Is hopeless.
Tho I would recognize your face
As the face that watches me writing poetry
In the restaurant downtown.

Such a strange feeling. Last night in the
Doorway of the bedroom
Unmasked; watching me dream you like we
Share an unresolved past.

Odd, I could not see you. Just a shadow lurking.

Warrior Going Strong

Warrior going strong
All painted up
Pays to have kept Dog-Soldier company
Lighting a smudge before battle
Draws you from your hiding spot

You don't look so brave now
In the middle of my sacred circle
Shakes you up how I keep hypnotic drum time
Swooping down   closing in
Gracefully manoeuvring my eagle landing
Almost sad to ruffle you with these powerful wings
Perched on your heart   beating out my victory song

Snag Poem

seducing me from a safe distance
a dark lover   so clever
dream eyes cosy up
want to be my nichimoose
say would you be satisfied just snuggling close
would suit me fine to blow this beer joint
so just keep lookin' sweetie
we'll jump the moon
kiss the stars
one big smile will do it

Private Thoughts on a Warm Night

Your body is cool, sensual, perfect to the touch
this wilting heatwave makes it impossible to sleep
just lay there thinking back to earlier tonight
your thirsting eyes drank me in,
what we could do if I'd invited you
up for tea, some slow-moving music
we're not sure   have to play it by ear
maybe just smile a lot, pretend we don't sneak peeks
but we know better   it's a matter of timing
silence   private thoughts are worth more unspoken
even when the mind races ahead
doesn't know where to begin   I start with the top
button   work my way down slowly   letting it just
happen   don't go too quickly save it & have some
special feeling to remember   like waves drenching my
body   while the moon swells to twice its normal size

Letter To Dean

The dreams fragment too easily,
break up
like sheets of ice, melting
into a vast river
to the unknown.

Now they have gone, the last one
I struggle to remember

what is it you're trying to say?
I see you searching for yourself
in the world
of the walking wounded.
You do not belong here.
This environment is stagnant,
an eventual graveyard
for the unsuspecting.

The smell of spilt beer,
the fraying fears choke the air.
But you will survive
the blood stains
and blackened eyes. In retrospect,
it will all be forgiven,
even the guy you bounced last night.

Dean, I do not understand these dreams
or the waiting between us:
we will carry on to the unseen end.
Perhaps then,
we will resume in a free, bloodless space.

Tonight, I think of my own frozen abilities,
and where you have gone

to the corners of my soul,
waiting to reappear next dream moon full.

June 17, 1992

His Own Private Jungle

From the darkness, safely hidden in black, curious
thoughts make cautious panther movements. His
tracks he brushes away so no trace can be found. But I
think jaguar, observing each well-kept secret.

After three months being a regular here, I hunger
to solve this mystery, to figure out who is haunting
who, & why. I need to see an elder, get direction. Since
making my tobacco offering, everything's on hold. The
nights are dreamless, but finally, I have rest.

He has a story he needs to tell. Sending a message
from the shadows, I want to give his loneliness back—
free myself. Talking with him, I see how carefully
he minds his own private jungle.

Scenes From A Passing Truck

The engine turns over, chokes again,
starts defiantly.

We keep driving, but where?
Someone is crying in the back. I
want to stop, find out why. Goddamn it,
that kid is howling now. PULL OVER!

Nothing but the motor humming, and
darkness. The headlights catch a
phantom movement out there—
p-a-s-s-i-n-g, gone.

I have grown into the seat. Your
eyes have become two jaguar moons.

Pressing your finger to my mouth, as
if to silence my screaming thoughts,
you trace my lips knowing this dream
will pass too quickly.

The engine dies. The child wakes me.

Night Visitor

A dark silhouette dances   across the wall
   Slips
through the sinew weaving of my dream-web
right into another dimension
   Haunting
those hands crave to make contact   they
want to reach inside me   pull out every
secret emotion
   Last night
those eyes so sad   I saw tears welling
brushed them away   kissing fragile my
phantom lover stole one more before waking
   Tonight
I find you upstairs
   Waiting to whisper
what was chasing you the night before last

Too Much Time

Time creeping up on me
I look like an old geezer
my face pressed up against the mirror
worrying my hairline even farther back
double panic: I don't know any bald Indians
my age   should be grateful I'm not a skinhead
tho part white   I'm not a racist
so I'm okay
but won't excuse these sinking eyes   to think
I used to get by on four hours   more like the
whole day now   barely crawling out of bed
doing an elder's routine
throw on my sweats   head to a park to write
only thing reminding me I'm not half dead:
those come-on looks

That Barren Season

for M.W.

Who could ever forget   that barren season
So dry & wasting
On the beach
My scribbler remained untouched   a drop
Of emotion would have been a godsend
Even to dive beneath waves
Would save me from another night   slumming
So easy to fall through a crack
On the street   lost
Letting you carve me up again
Those blood spots told a story   after the
Party   crawling on me
Picking over bones   So bare & bleached
Escaping   at dawn
To the sea   I couldn't squeeze out one poem
I was happy with

Another Slow Night

Each glimmering fantasy arranged for quick, easy
    reference
Lying safe with his nichimoose in the darkness
Each one has a secret to share
Cuddling up, whispers tickle inside his ears

These early hours bring them to his level
Projecting alone, he's gotten good travelling at night
Once he even slipped back to a medieval time
Saved his tower-kept lover from sure suicide

Dreaming the nights away, he has his regulars
Every moving exchange gets recorded for future trips
Some he is more secretive about, using poetry to hide
    behind
The guise of abstract thinking

His trunk is filled with scraps of paper
Collecting over the years, he just keeps on writing
Capturing each ghostly lover like a snapshot
He'll go back & reread them, saying, "Was I really
    that lonely?"

Smudge Ceremony

A Spider's Delicate Work

A spider's delicate work   hangs in mind   an endless
thread   weaving me into his sticky tapestry   unravels
my dreams   shamelessly

crawl back into my abalone smudge bowl
sage smoke going up high
summons an eagle circling
circling
hands through smoke wash head
face
shoulders
back
stomach
legs
feet

purified   ready to chase him
under his own black creation

The Process

Run off to sleep
Packing my ragged book of poems
Keep me tossing nights
Shooting down senseless words   matchless stanzas
One huge puzzle   trying to piece myself together

I want to cry   scream my way out of this protective
Shell   unbreakable   so many years conditioning
These soft spots   only too ready to take another blow

Still   the words come a lot easier since I quit drinking
I dream of poetry
It comes from a sacred birthing place

South / Healing

Count Yourself Lucky

Twentieth Street
Sure remember cheap draft.
Each glass gave a temporary cure.
Hocking the TV
Got a couple of pitchers.
And my dancing outfit: we stayed
Cut for a whole week.
(Indian tradition to share the wealth)
When the shakes start up, you got to
Pool your resources.
No haggling over who put in more. Just
Count yourself lucky to be getting a buzz.

Too Snug

Even I get too snug in the good life
Roaming Vancouver's ugly side,
I forget the feel of my cushion
Down-&-outers ask for change
Most would hurry off, disgusted
by what they see
I give two-bits & a smoke, knowing it's
a prayer
I don't need to hear a hard-up story
to be a do-gooder
Just remembering mine is good enough
I made my welfare cheque stretch,
not like these old-timers
They know how to survive
Talking you up for cash,
maybe even a glass of draft
if you have the time of day.

Intact

Weather-beaten but intact
This petroglyph of some long-ago world
Etched in mind   Sink back breathing
Your body   Clean & fresh
Like rain on the skids   Drumming out
Those jungle noises
Pounding
Safe in arms   Seducing me under with
Fingers smooth   Tracing circles
Boring past my protective layer
Deeper   Dismantling me thoughtlessly
Scattered   Forgotten to drunken bed-spins
And the blackness of your numbed world

I Was Here, Once

My city hunger is quickly fed its fill.
Coming back to the strip, what memory surfaced?

They don't know it, but I was here, once.
Even then, there was no place to go.
Just the all-night coffee shop down in Hookerville.

The clientele never changes. They die off or
Move to another city. Few are lucky enough
To get out, like me. Still, there is always
Something dragging you back.

What is it for me, these lost kids? They should be
Home, not with Johns. I want to give society
An overhaul, clean the streets of every ball-less pimp.

If I was God, hard to say what I'd do first. In
The end, I'd exile them to an island called
Their conscience.
The rest would be history, never to be repeated—
Only remembered by those who survived.

At Wounded Knee

Beneath earth & grass
History is buried   Wind carries
Remnants of the past
Ghost-Chanting across the plains
Bones
Deep down
Hidden & twisted
Underfoot

The dark sky is genuine enough—
No poetry, there is an emptiness
So vast my heart echoes
Beating, slows, becomes still

Frozen like Bigfoot's corpse
White visitors have trouble with this monument
Not with the past, but the crushed
Beer cans left by modern-day warriors
I had to wonder if those tourists
Heard the spirit-women
Keening

All in the Interpretation

All in the interpretation
Churchgoing
Only Christmastime
That's it for me
Feels odd making my genuflection
Chanting
More natural to use sweetgrass
Cleaned up the old way
Put my spirit in the right place

Praying on knees
An entire generation
Scarred
Senseless hailing Mary
So full of our disgrace
Refused to hear us
After the lights went out
God's hands went to work

Behind This Barricade

Behind this barricade of dead-falls and razor wire
We tighten our circle
Calling our old ones with
Sweetgrass prayers
Heads bowed
The passing of
Silence
an eagle feather moves from warrior to woman
To warrior to woman
Chanting

A different ceremony on the other side
News reporters broadcast the movements
of camouflaged wolves
Pointing semi-automatics
into living rooms across the country

Face to face
We might learn something if we stop long enough
to hear that Mohawk sisters' account
of how stones break more than bones.

Speaking Real Indian

Chalk this one up to a learning lesson
Damn nervy using me as your surrogate voice
CBC must look pretty impressive on that resume
Claiming the honour
Like a wolf after guts

Me, I'm counting coup the old-fashioned way; stalking
Your dreams
Even Grey Owl & Long Lance
Couldn't master that technique
Tho sure sneaky fooling the public

Who would ever guess
You had a ghost writer doctoring your speech
Speaking real Indian
Is a true-red talent
No white writer talk that good Cree

Instant Power

Perched outside her window
a grandmother in crow guise
Laughing
No wonder   That pipe she picked up

Last summer at the powwow
Hunting craft tables for just the right bag
She lucked out—a real steal for two bucks
So excited   Had to show off her new treasure

She didn't notice the bowl was missing   Hmmm....
Big mystery
But some dancer found it   She thanked him with
A braid of sweetgrass   Good honour

Tho she's pissed off with my explanation
Acquiring instant power will end up worthless
Take my advice sister
That grandmother will keep you rolling nights

New Council Old Words

The justice building downtown
Seeing more Indian action these days
Just like our old-time councils
Coming from far and wide   to sacred ground
Now the city
Getting the message out
Not with moccasin power or smoke   but camcorder
Zooming in on elders drumming   nice to see
We're sticking to tradition
At home   following the proceedings via satellite
Transport the Indian way   adjust my antenna   fine-
Tuned   slip through the screen   on the scene
Supporting the GitKsan   clan chief marking out
Eagle territory
Road block visitors who never left   I like that
Definition   how the word "inherent" rolls off
The tongue   outdoing those Mac Blo lawyers
Just White Paper talking again   It's the eloquence
Of Indian speech that carries that truth   Earth poetry
Gushing from lips   Not every word pointing to the
Judge's clear-cut decision

Between Sides

Where do I belong, way up north?
The first white trader
Must have felt this way

    on the reserve   a curio being looked over
    my skin defies either race   I am neither Scottish
    or Cree

So why those disgusted stares?
I speak the language
Eat my bannock with lard

    I am not without history   Halfbreed labour built
    this country   defending my blood has become a
    life-long occupation

White people have their own ideas
How a real Indian should look
In the city or on the screen

    I've already worked past that   came back to the
    circle   my way is not the Indian way or white way

I move in-between
Careful not to shame either side

Answer For My Brother

Who Are The Métis?

His question   a clever way to get me thinking where
is my place but I detect something else because he's
an Indian having been through the wringer   only he
came out with a strong sense of self   going to back to
the sacred teachings

My writing is no comparison but I write to heal so I
find sacredness in the captured thought which brings
me to all the volumes written about Indians be that
pre-history or prophetic insights that will lead us into
the future   but

There is so little written about the Métis because we
are not one or the other   but a shaded combination
that is easier to figure out   lumping all of us
together because some Halfbreeds look like they have a
dark past which to

The outsider appears an Indian past & then there are
some so white you wouldn't think twice   they have an
immigrant history even tho they gave birth to the
Province Manitoba getting the short end of the stick
because greedy land

Grabbers wanted the whole damn country
so whoever looked dark enough got treaty covering up
their tainted blood & thier not-so-passable cousins
were sent packing to the backwoods being written
right out of history   except for

Brief mention of our leaders   who were a thorn in the
government's ass   they made it to the N section in the
encyclopedia under the "North West Rebellion"
which more or less infers we needed to be put into our
proper place

Which might as well have been a zoo because the city
is a zoo & we're on display at your local beer joint
talking about uncle Gabe & buffalo-hunting days
which was the very essence of our survival   even tho
Indian politicians claim compensation for each &
every buffalo   we never forgot the hungry years.

If anything, we are Katipamsoochick.

Making New History

Making new history
Columbus bashing is passe
Insider secret: we all grew up on bannock & baloney
No shame here
Uncle Tomahawk working hard to cut off those
In between Indians
Don't fit the blood criteria
But expect us to support your constitutional demands
In limbo
Out back your reserve
Squatting
On road allowance
Those better-than stares
Looking down on us
We're still homeless
Ironic
We all got screwed
Five hundred years later: a new Half-breed rebellion
Brewing

Good Sweating

Round One: enter womb sun-wise   minding prayers
offer my tobacco to heated stones
remember to be grateful   fix my eyes to
darkness   when the door flap closes
water on stones   hissing

Round Two: bear down on heat wave   changes in
breathing   prickles   skin boring holes
release impurities of mind   body
spirit cleansed

Round Three: melt to cool earth   against my face
laying still   take in grandmothers
grandfathers singing   join voices
become one

Round Four: exit womb sun-wise   hiy-hiy
all my relations   reborn

Sour Note

This note's for you
with a jab   I might add
subtracting out of loyalty
the faithful years
so not to numb you out totally

my nerves scream inside
you're so damn hard

I want my friendship back
pull out, forget
I'm still pliable
(even healing is no excuse)

say this was me
to you
dumping my garbage
is another poem   even then
I wouldn't walk away
smelling sweet

as for the past
and all our secrets
I'm too far along
to betray you

it's vanishing on a sour note—
your rotting silence
when I need an ear

Today

You're in this dream of endless water.   An under-
Current struggles against my waking.
I worry about the message.   What if we're slowly
Dying, isn't that how it always happens?

But it's the absence of words; how we keep drowning
In each other's silence that tells me we'll survive.
Like the sea, we will endure to the end.   And that
Is the whole mystery.   How can we keep afloat,
Appear so peaceful on the surface when we know deep
Down the sea is hungry?

In the end, our hearts will betray us.   Your eyes
Have since given out; revealing an emptiness so vast
I would be grateful sinking to the bottom.   But I
Cannot desert you & I don't know why.

Remembering the tears,
Your heart pounding out an S–O–S, I get caught once
Again.   It's the downward spiral that terrifies me.   I
Don't want to think too much today.

The Spirits Have Begun Working

My steel bones have been replaced with glass; a
Jagged edge
Works against even the slightest movement

>   the spirits have begun working   in dreams
>   last night   my face got painted   divided by
>   a thin black line   yellow on one side   four
>   black dots on cheek

It is lodged in-between my shoulder blades,
Shifting as I move around the wheel   only the
Degree of pain changes without consent

>   an old woman was soothing me in Cree   I
>   cried in her lap   she kept singing   singing
>   an old man gave me four eagle feathers   four
>   songs   four stories   then painted my face
>   divided in two

This morning comes cloudy,
Reminds me I'm fragile, healing,
Too human

Glossary

Dog Soldier   A select Cheyenne warrior society that was noted for their bravery and courage.

Dream-web   A circular hoop with spider-like webbing which serves as a filter to good and bad dreams.

Hiy-hiy   Denotes thankfulness, said after prayers.

Kachina   Hopi, Zuni and Pueblo male dancers who impersonate Spirit Beings; also wooden figurines which are representations of the masked dancers.

Katipamsoochick   The people who own themselves.

Keemootch   Sly, or sneaky.

Kiyas   A long time ago.

Kohkum   Grandmother.

Moshom   Grandfather.

Nimis   Sister.

Nichimoose   Sweetheart.

Skin   A term first introduced by the American Indian Movement to describe native heritage or nativeness.

Smudge   A ceremony to purify one's body, mind and spirit.

Sweetgrass   A braided fragrant grass used in most native ceremonies, particularly among Plains tribes.

Tobacco Offering   A sacred offering made before prayer or before requesting advice from an elder or a spiritual person.

Uncle Tomahawk   A corrupt native organization and its administrators.

Note   Cree words used in this book have been spelled in their anglicized form.